Mind's Labyrinth

In the Silence of Thought

Niharika Chauhan

BookLeaf Publishing

India | USA | UK

Acknowledgement

As I reflect on the journey that brought these poems to life, I am filled with gratitude for those who have been an integral part of this quiet exploration.

To my family and friends: your unwavering support has been the quiet strength behind every word I've written. Your understanding and encouragement have helped me embrace my inner voice, even when it was soft and uncertain.

To the mentors and teachers who have guided me through moments of doubt and discovery: your wisdom and insight have been invaluable. You have shown me that finding my voice doesn't require volume, but rather a deep, authentic connection to who I am.

And to all the silent warriors out there, navigating your own paths of self-discovery and coping with your inner turmoil: this book is a testament to our shared experience. May it remind you that you are not alone and that even in the quietest moments, your strength and impact are profound.

Preface

In a world that often equates volume with significance and visibility with worth, finding one's voice can be an overwhelming challenge. This collection of poems is a reflection on the quiet strength that lies beneath the surface, a testament to the power of inner resolve and the profound impact of actions over words.

As a young person navigating the complexities of self-discovery, I have come to realize that being heard doesn't always require raising your voice. Sometimes, the most profound messages are conveyed in the hushed spaces between our thoughts, in the subtlety of our actions, and in the stillness of our hearts. This collection captures those moments of quiet introspection and the struggle to reconcile inner turmoil with the desire to make a meaningful impact.

These poems are born from the realization that finding your true self is a journey marked by silence as much as by expression. They explore the delicate balance between speaking out and listening in, between showing strength and embracing vulnerability. Each verse is a step towards understanding that true power often lies in the ability to remain steadfast and authentic, even when the world around us seems to demand more.

To those who, like me, grapple with the challenge of expressing what often feels unutterable, these pages are for you. They are a reminder that the essence of who we are is not defined by the noise we make but by the quiet integrity of our actions and the strength of our inner selves. Herein lies a celebration of the silent yet powerful journey towards self-realization, a journey that proves one need not be the loudest in the room to be heard, and that coping with one's inner struggles is both a personal victory and a testament to enduring strength.

May these words offer solace, inspiration, and a gentle reminder that even in the quietest moments, our voices can resonate with profound impact.

Whirlwind of Thoughts

In the stillness of my room
Where the shadows gently loom
My mind's a stormy sea
A mirror to chaos, wild and free

Often I wish my mind
Could mirror the room's serene quiet
To match its calm
And shield itself from the turmoil's riot

If only I could press a button
To release my mind
From the racing thoughts
That blaze and unwind

If only it were that simple
Everyone would seek
But if all our problems vanished
How would life's journey speak?

Unveiling of the Soul

In the silence of thought where shadows
blend
The mind finds peace where echoes mend
A stillness blooms as voices fade
And quiet whispers softly cascade

In moments hushed, where thoughts are slow
Deep currents stir, and secrets show
Not through clamor nor the rush of sound
But in the calm where truths are found

The conscious mind takes a gentle pause
Unraveling the tangled laws
And in this silence, pure and clear
Insight and wisdom reappear

It's here, amid the quiet's grace
That clarity begins to trace
A path unseen, yet deeply known
Where the heart's true wisdom is gently sown

So listen close when thoughts retreat
In silent spaces answers meet
For in the stillness of the mind
The deepest truths are often signed

Beyond the Veil of Storms

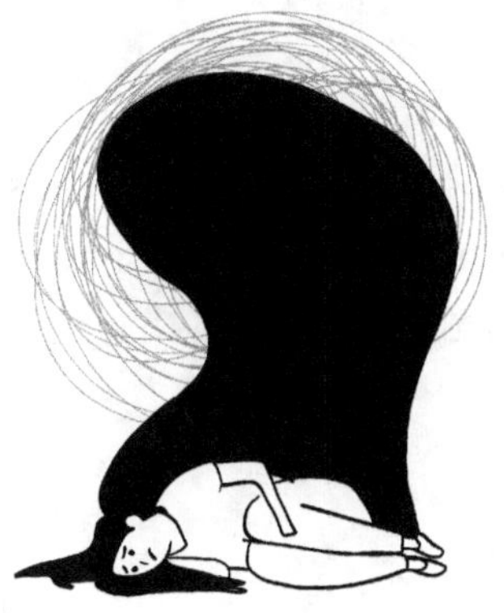

Sometimes I feel like a shadowed storm
Swirling in darkness, taking fierce form
Wishing for someone to calm the fight
To lift me from behind this veil of night

If you looked closer you'd truly see
The soul beneath this storm is me
Please, don't turn away as others do
Like fleeing a storm that looms in view

For inside the chaos, there's a quiet space
A hidden refuge, a peaceful place
I'm not as tangled as I seem to be
I'm not a storm; there's more to me

I'm a story yet to unfold, unread
A book with pages still unsaid
So stay a while, take time to see
The calm and depth that lies in me

Echoes of Silence

In the stillness of a silent room
Where whispers fall and shadows loom
The quiet mind begins to weave
A tapestry of thoughts that breathe

Unspoken words, like fleeting sighs
Drift softly through the tranquil skies
And in the hush where echoes stay
The past and present gently play

Memories like echoes call
Soft reverberations faint but tall
Their voices blend with inner light
Shaping visions in the night

Though silence wraps its gentle cloak
The silent mind's echo speaks and strokes
In muted tones, it softly shows
The depth of feeling no one knows

So in the quiet listen close
To the subtle pulse that softly flows
For in the stillness, thoughts reside
With echoes vast and deep inside

The Awakening

If I make a sound, I'm seeking the light
If I stay silent, I'm lost in the night
Oh dear God please hear my plea
It's hard to be helped when no one can see

Why must I strive to please them all?
Why does every step lead to my fall?
But why should their whims govern my fate?
I wasn't born to carry their weight

This life is a gift to wander and roam
To feel nature's kiss, to find my true home
It's never too late to start anew
Never say never—your journey's for you

The Dilemma of Desire and Fulfillment

All I desire is to be heard, to be seen, to be
esteemed
Yet when attention graces me, why do I feel as
though I should retreat behind the scenes?
When I am overwhelmed by abundance
I find myself longing for anonymity

In the face of plenty, I am unsettled
And in its absence, discontent also takes hold
Why is it that life's offerings never satisfy our
quest for contentment?
Why can we not embrace what is given
And transform it into something more liven?

The Paradox of Being Seen

In a crowd yet feeling so alone
I wonder if someone out there is my own
Attention comes from every side
Yet the one I seek seems to hide

Why, when longing for a gaze
Does my presence fade from view
And why, when I wish for solitude's embrace
Does the spotlight shine so brightly too

Obligation towards trust

Like glass so fragile takes so much time to
build
Broken in a second unfeasible to be pieced
Not ever is it treated with delicacy
When it must be regarded with constancy

Something so personal shared with perplexity
Sorrowful how it's corrupted so easily
With love and care shall we perceive
A bond so pure yet easy to deceive

Timeline of Smile

All day, a smile remains consistent
Just as the sun rays so radiant
Starting morning, till the night
They continue to unfurl their light

Soon when evening befalls
Rays begin to take a shortfall
Smoke and darkness unfold and blend
Concurrently smile and light descends

The Weight of Blame

You blame me for the pain you feel
But what of wounds that never heal
It's easy, isn't it, to say my name
And pin me down beneath your shame

But what of the hurt you've left in me
The scars you cause that none can see
I wish to erase the bitter past
To let go of the shadows you cast

Yet you make it hard to forgive, forget
Your actions linger my soul in debt
If only I could undo the day
When fate led me to you that way

I wish I'd never known your face
Or met you in that fateful place
Oh, how I long for a chance anew
A life where I could start without you

The Passage of Time

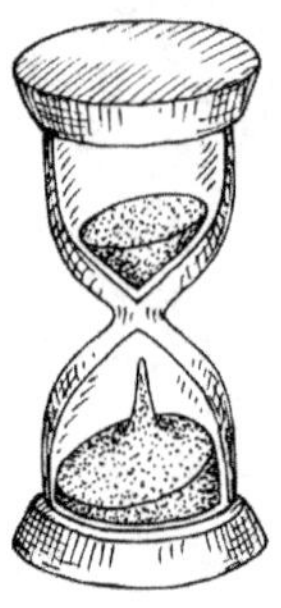

Like day giving way to the cloak of night
Time slips away, an elusive flight
We hardly notice as moments blend
How we grow older how changes descend

Responsibilities weigh like unseen chains
Some joys ignite, while some leave stains
A crazy phenomenon, this ebb and flow
Each day we age yet seldom know

Look how small we were, so innocent, free
Innocence lost yet longing to see
Something stirs deep within my soul
A whirlwind of feelings out of control

Overwhelmed by the pace this journey so vast
Reflecting on moments both present and past
Each tick of the clock, a bittersweet thrill
In the dance of life, we embrace the still

For My Mother

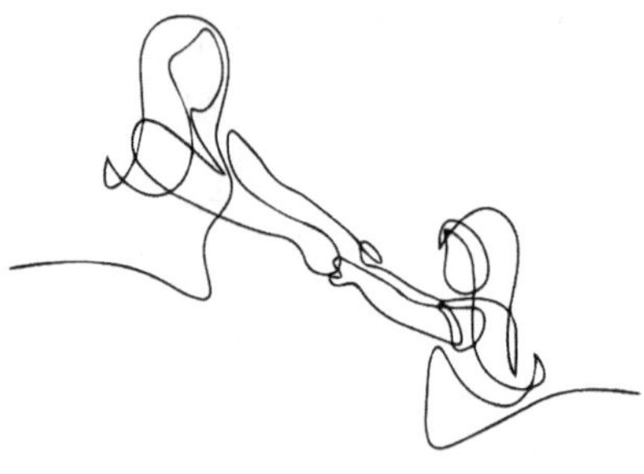

You take my pain, you feel my joy
In every moment, you're my ploy
You give your all, and ask for naught
A gift more rare than heaven's sought

I ask for nothing, just your stay
My dearest friend, in every way
My soulmate, anchor, all in one
With you, my battles are always won

I hope you know though words may fall
How much you mean—my heart, my all
Love you, mother, forever true
In all I am I owe to you

For My Father

You're my anchor, Steadying me
Any time of the day, You're there for me
Through the plight, through the dark
You always lit up my spark

Even if times were at their worst
You have always put me first
Time may pass by in its swiftness
But I'll forever be your little princess

No words can express my gratitude
A silent symphony of the heart's latitude
Thank you for every step that you guide
You will forever be my greatest pride

Birthdays

Everyone's happy the air's alive
Excitement bubbles as we all thrive
This one special day where sorrows take flight
A celebration of you, everything feels right

The best feeling of the entire year
With laughter and love and those we hold
dear
You stand in the spotlight the world in your
hand
Birthday lights twinkle as joy takes a stand

Colors abound a vibrant display
As poppers burst forth in a festive ballet
Confetti cascades a shower of cheer
In this magical moment, your heart feels so
near

So here's to the laughter, the cake, and the
song
To the love that surrounds you, where you
belong
For today is a treasure, so bright and so clear
Happy birthday dear one, it's your day

The Power of Emotions

You lift us high, you make us strong
You stir our hearts, a constant song
You make us laugh, you make us weep
A force that runs so vast, so deep

In every choice, you guide the way
You color each and every day
You hold the power, great and true
In every mood, in all we do

From joy to sorrow, fear to grace
You shape the soul, you leave your trace
Emotions, you, the silent guide
The pulse of life we cannot hide

NYE

As twilight dims and stars come out
We gather together, filled with doubt
A year of laughter, lessons embraced
Each moment cherished, every joy faced

The countdown calls, excitement in view
With hopes and dreams, we welcome the new
As the clock strikes twelve, colors explode
A brand new year, our spirits bestowed

So here's to the journey, new paths to find
New times, new thoughts, leave the past
behind

The Ties that Forever Last

In the heart of our home, love finds its way
A tapestry woven, where memories play
Through laughter and tears, in joy and in pain
Family is the anchor that helps us remain

Each voice is a harmony each smile a spark
In the darkest of times they light up the dark
So here's to the moments, both great and
serene
For family is the treasure, our bond evergreen

The Ever-Changing Sky

You shift your colors, change your form
Yet always stay, through calm and storm
Forever here, you never part
A constant witness to the heart

Sometimes you rage, in tempest wild
But mostly calm, serene and mild
Oh sky, you are a wondrous sight
A canvas kissed by day and night

You guide us through the passing time
Or are those moods that shift, sublime?
In you, we see the world unfold
A story, timeless, yet untold

A Gentle Presence

I have someone always by my side
In every mood, a quiet guide
Not just a shadow, but a friend so near
A comforting whisper that calms my fear

It doesn't always mean the dark or the dread
For in their presence I'm gently led
Perhaps we share a bond unseen
Transforming the world where love can glean

Maybe it's not bad; maybe it's bright
A spirit that dances in soft twilight
Together we laugh together we roam
In this sacred space I'm never alone

So let the world think what it may
For in this companionship, I find my way
With every heartbeat, I learn to embrace
The beauty of ghosts in a warm, safe place

Eternal Brilliance

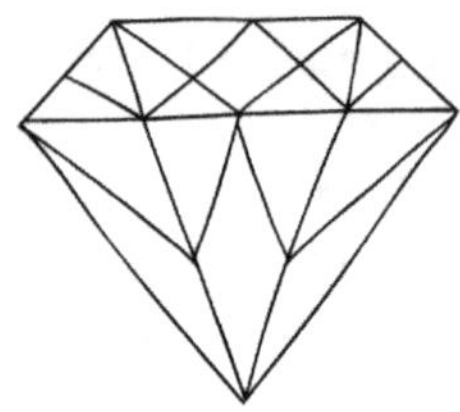

You shimmer bright, you glow with grace
A spark of joy in every place
You turn the dull into something rare
A touch of beauty, light as air

With all the power the world can hold
You gleam in hues of silver and gold
So radiant, so pure, so clear
A gem that all are drawn to near

Illuminating, fresh, divine
No one can ever claim enough of your shine
You lift the heart you light the way
A diamond glowing night and day

A Beauty Beyond Compare

You are the most beautiful thing I've known
A wonder in every form you've shown
With countless variations, so surreal
A beauty so vast, it's hard to feel real

How lucky am I to live in a space
Where your presence makes the world a grace
You turn the earth to a heavenly place
With every change, each subtle trace

So many forms, so many hues
In every way, you bring something new
Yet no matter how you choose to appear
Your beauty is constant, always near

An Ode to the Green

So green you gleam, a vibrant sheen
Your scent, a joy, a breath serene
You shield us from the storm and sun
Guardians when the day's undone

You help us breathe you help us live
To nature's grace your life you give
You make this world a place of grace
A beauty none can dare replace

For all you do we owe you much
A better world through your soft touch

For My Constant

We've grown side by side, hand in hand
With laughter as light as a loud band
Through teasing jests and playful fights
We always found our way to make it right

I've seen you shine I've seen you fall
Through every phase I've known it all
We danced in joy we wept in pain
Through every storm through sun and rain

No words could capture what you mean
In you my constant soul has been
All these years, and still we stand
Heart to heart and hand in hand

So here's to birthdays yet to come
No distance great no journey done
No matter where no matter when
Forever you'll be my best of friends

Happy birthday, my forever constant
Our hearts stay bound, though life moves on
Here's to your 18th birthday